VERSES UNRAVELED

RECONNECTING YOU TO THE WORLD OF POETRY

KALYAN KUMAR
ANUSHKA YADAV

Made with ♥ on the Notion Press Platform
www.notionpress.com

Contents

"Poetry is a sword of lightning, ever unsheathed, which consumes the scabbard that would contain it"

    - Percy Bysshe Shelley.

Author

Kalyan Kumar is one of the most renowed writers in the world currently. He has won 3 International Bestseller Awards in Germany,Australia and New York in 3 consecutive years. Currently he is the brand ambassador of New York Publication. He is known as a get poet and a stroyteller. He has also been featured on Book of world records. This is his 13th book overall.

Joining him is a young Co-Author Anushka Yadav From Uttar Pradesh India. This is her debut book.

The World

The world of which you dreamed of
Or the world that is so mean,
The world you were told about
Or the world you have seen.

They are sugar coated
With the venom of snakes,
They are pretty toxic
With the words and the phrase.

They pretent to be happy
When they are not,
bright glowing face
who are self-centred from the soul.

The world is full of darkness
Darkness with the pain untold,
This is the reality of the world
Which cannot be controlled.

The inner mess of mine
That was never being told,
The fireflies that I followed
I followed them till home!!

I Wanna Talk

I wanna talk to you
Cause maybe I'm feeling left alone,
I wanna talk to you
Cause maybe I'm dreaming on my own.

I wanna talk to you
Cause maybe I am finding a source of light,
I also need someone,who can talk to me
On that moonlight night.

I wanna talk to you
Because everyday I fall asleep crying,
Maybe I'm good at hiding
But from inside I am really just dying.

I am good at hiding tears
I am on all ears,
So tell me what you have been hiding
From past so many years.

Tell me,if you don't
Have words to describe,
I am good at listening silence
And the words of divine.

I wanna talk to you
Where the silence occurs the place,
Where we can understand ourselves
And our talk will remain the same.

Once I Am Gone

Once I am gone you'll search for me
Madly in your way once I am gone,
You'll be shattered in pieces
And cursing for fading away.

Just once let me leave,pray for my death
Cause I don't want you to,
Stay awake the whole night
And search for my soul instead.

Once I'll be gone,
I'll never look back,
I'll become the mystery
And will leave not a single track.

You'll cry in my absence
You'll look for my attention,
Oh darling! just once if I'll be gone
Then to whom will you show your aggression?

I know you are not like that
I know that wasn't your intention,
And usually I don't disappear
But my love this is the case of exception.

I'll close my eyes
To be never opened again
Placing my hands, Near my heart
And would be screaming in pain.

Remember that if I'll be gone
Then there would be no acceptance,
for sorry and pain and no other way
To regret your doing except my grave.

It will be better if I'll be gone
And leaving no memories to stay,
But once I am gone then just dont come behind
Following me on the way.

Incoherent Situation

I have poems written inside me
That the paper could not handle,
Am I searching for the path
In the dark without a candle?

Am I wrong that I expected much
Or Am I choosing the wrong way to go?
What if I also get indulged in the darkness
Will the things remain the same though ?

Am I looking for peace
Or am I following the echoes, throughout the dark?
What if humans do not have darkness inside them
What if we lighten up the world so far?

I am in the dilemma
To stay or to walk away,
How confusing it is
Just to choose the correct way.

Let your darkness
Stay in the dark,
Just step out
From the world of black hours.

Is it correct to let the things

Be left as they are,

Cause I was already bleeding

Throughout my whole past.

Ephmeral

When I reached there
I saw that you were already gone,
And I have no idea
How to move on.

You should have told me
If anything went wrong,
Because maybe I am just
Not being able to hold it on.

I was just remembering
Of those beautiful days,
Now just tell me how I'm gonna
Survive in these lost ways.

The expectations I had
I had it by mistake,
Now I am playing reckless
When my life is at stake.

I have deep sarrows
And same unnecessary loudness in my mind,
They told me that my mind
Must be a terrible place during all that time.

You made my life living hell
And I suffered it all with a smile,
You should have told me that you don't care
Cause for me that would be fine... !!

Mixed Thoughts

She was awake
In the stillness of night,
She loves darkness
But also searches for light.

You were the only one
Who lighted up my world,
Are you really leaving me now
When you know that I'm at my worst.

I'm ready to be ignored
And to be avoided all the time,
But just assure me the you are gonna stay
Always by my side.

I told you about my heart
Where it hurts,
And you made me bleed colourlessly
So perfectly at first.

You made bleed from my eyes,
And still expecting me to be mine,
Why it is always called as weeping
But not bleeding from eyes.

I stood up from my bed
And went to the table to write
But however I was just not able,
To find the words to describe.

I spend whole night
Looking at the paper
But however my mind become empty,
And the paper remained white !!

What We Call As Life

When I woke up from my bed
I found everything magical
Which I can feel around me
Every single sight of mine,
Was like a fascinating dream.

It was all beautiful
Green leaves,blue skies
Sun sets and sun rise
And there were many more to look for,
Without blinking my eyes.

However everything was as good
Everything was fine
But I don't know
Why it felt like,
As if it is the last day of mine.

I met my friends
And had a lot of fun
And when I looked at my watch
It was already,
The time for the sun to set.

So,I went to a high place
To look for the sunset
With a good sight
I was spending my time in serenity,
But suddenly my body felt light.

I don't remember
Why I started crying
But I saw my body fading away
Leaving me behind,
With the cruel time.

To give it a check
I ran towards my home
And stood still with numbers inside
And felt that my heart,
Was really broke that night.

It didn't made any sound
But could be felt
That it was shattered
Just like a crystal,
Made up of ice.

I don't know why
The girl who was lying on the floor
Was looking similar to me

I don't know why she was giving me,
A familiar vibe.

I saw my parents
Crying upon my deadbody
I saw myself sleeping with,
Happiness inside.

Two stages of emotions
Sorrow and happiness ,that are abide
It is all,
What we humans call as life..?

The Ashes Of The Burnt Heart

Darkness is not scary
But we humans are
They are the one
Who removes the covering
And ask you again,
About that same old scar.

Humans are the one
To hit and scratch
And scratch and rub
The wounds which I have been hiding,
To several years from last.

Stabbing me every single time
Whenever I started to believe again
Leaving me half dead,
With shadow of black hours.

Judging you for your colour
And how capable you are
Making you feel low
In every step you take,
So that if you fall you can fall more hard.

Words are not ugly
But we human are
With the changing tones
And the masks they mold
They the ones,
Why I am so cold.

Leaving her behind
She was left all alone
No one is around her
Only her shivering in the cold
Is it all the people have learnt,
From those ancient quotes.

Making her heart
A terrible place to stay
Filled with hatred, jealousy
And demons outraged.

The melancholy darkness
That resides inside me
Wanting me to take revenge,
For my every defeat.

Crying and shivering
Shivering and scratching

Scratching her harshly
Till the blood comes out
Making her quiet,
When she was not even loud.

I was scratching myself
And you made me love to do it
Until all the blood of my body,
Got vapourized.

Then my ribs were visible
As all of my skin was scratched
And the blood which was once red,
Slowly turned into wine.

Then I will realised
That my heart was black
Was it already black
From the very beginning
Or it was being burnt
During all that time..!!

The Red Art

I was in a museum
And it attracted my sight so far
There were not any colour except red
And no paint brushes,
Just some objects that were sharp.

I got lost in that evil painting
As it has taken over me and being me
I was turned silent,
While looking at that masterpiece.

It made me quite
I was forced to think about it
And there were so many questions,
That were going inside my head.

The burden that the words hold
To be said and to be carved
And in instant I realised
The weight which I was holding
Was nothing but the weight of the memories,
That I still carry from my past.

It was difficult for me
To speak or to laugh

As my skin emerging ,
With some new scars.

There were also some cuts
Suming as someone has drawn
His life on my skin,
With a Knife.

As I can see,
They were fresh and bleeding
All red on the book,
Which I was reading.

The pain which was there
Was nothing infront of the pain
That was in my heart,
How can I get distracted, just by a piece of art.

It was like a horrible dream
The stream which was beside me was a red stream
And when that dream over
I was still there in front of that cursed painting,
After that again my heart started to complaining.

That art had some words in it
The verse of broken hearts
To comfort the disturbed

And distrub the comfortable one's

If is all, what we humans

meant by art..?

Sorrow And Serenity

I choose to bleed on a white shirt
I chose to be lift alone and hallow
I chose to not to explicate my things,
I chose to dance in the rain of sorrow.

I will do the thing freely
Which haunts the townspeople
I will be there in the shadows,
Doing the things that are lethal.

You know what it feels so good
To get lost in the forest regardless of time
Walking beside a beautiful stream,
Not concerned about the safety of mine.

I am literally good here
With a little sorrow and some peace
I am fine with these wild animals,
I am happy with my grief.

Atleast I can talk here
I can talk to the winds
And can play with the water,
I can be my real self for so much longer.

Wild animals are not the things
Which terrifies me
Because if one is not loved exceptionally,
He must be the one who everyone fears.

Maybe these wild animals
Never felt loved our understood
I don't know why but I can relate to them,
For being so much cruel.

I was also misunderstood once
Misunderstood for no reason that's when I felt
That would is not the one which I dreamed of,
This is not the place where I could live.

Life Needs A Pause

Life needs a pause
Pull back the thread of chaos
Slump back the storms of emotions
Slow down the noise of your heart,
Shut down the tarnish windows of dejection.

And just sit around
An open ocean, wide and calm
Where your reflection blends
With an open sky and you are
All free to write the best
Episodes of your life.

Just knock off the abandon
Corridor of your nightmares
Where you walk alone, insane
Which screams the dreadful
Realities in the backyard of your brain.

Take a moment and breathe,
And build a sand castle of your dreams
Under the umbrella of starry night
Just you,winning your inner fight.

A Battle In Dreams

I thought it was real and fought with might
Blinded by weapons, lost in the fight
The more I struggled, the more I bled, Trapped in a war inside my
head
I chased the battle, raw and wild,
Yet every strike was fate beguiled.

I closed my eyes, embraced the night
But when I woke, the pain had died
No wounds remained, no scars to hide
For all was false-a fleeting dream
And as the end drew near my sight,
No dream shall dim these fearless eyes.

A shadowed war, not what it seemed
And in that dawn, my spirit soared
No nightmare rules what life has stored
My fate is mine, my soul will rise,
No dream shall dim these fearless eyes.

Himalayas My Cage

The more I walked

My bag got heavier, my feet sore,

My pace slow, my beat faster,

And my souls lighter.

I came to the mountains a free man but the path made me it's

prisoner.

The days were tiring and the nights sleepless.

The sun burnt me through my screens

And I felt every kiss of the chilly winds

But at the summit I knelt down and smiled.

Embers

It's in the whispered embers
Of everything said
Where our hearts traveled
The boughs of time together
Where your lips addressed
My being and soul
To the fire of life
It's the sonnet of a 1000 poets
Calling from the horizon
There in them
The dreams of lovers
The longing of hearts
Was the melody of you
I knew loves sweetness
Kissed deep it's passion
And drank of it's wine
You bore me away
Upon the fancy of dreams
Holding me tight
In your lullaby,
Through the night.

As A Broken Man

As the rain falls and the wind blows

I find myself with a smile so what I hold inside don't show

The things I wish no one to know

I wish not to be a burden

I know no one can help me not even the church or a sergeant

I feel as if I am damned

Here to rome this land

As a broken man.

Yet even though I may be broken

My words go without being unspoken

Even if inside I feel as if I am choking

I hide what I hold inside with that of joking

So you don't see the torment I go through, Things you are lucky

you never knew

And when I find myself distant just know I do still love you,

What I hold is all I have ever knew....

My Soul

In shadows deep
Where silence sags
I stand alone
Everyone's punching bag ,Words like fists
They sting and stab
Yet I endure.
The highly cruel jab. Bruised but resilient
My heart is pained,
I wish they knew My soul is maimed.

Indulgence In Chocolate

In the kitchen's warm embrace
A symphony of scents takes place
Cocoa whispers fill the air,
As chocolate cake begins to prepare.

Flour sifts like softest snow
As butter melts in gentle flow
Sugar crystals, pure and sweet,
Blend with eggs in a dance complete.

Into the oven, the batter goes
Where magic works as time slows
Rising high with tender care,
The cake emerges, beyond compare.

Rich and dark, a cocoa dream
Layers stacked, a chocolate stream
Velvet crumb and ganache gleam,
In each bite, a taste supreme.

With every forkful, hearts delight
In chocolate's embrace, spirits take flight
A slice of heaven, moist and fine,
Chocolate cake, forever divine.

Clutching Of Palms

Gentle clutching of palms
Slip your fingers in the gaps of mine
Feel the softness turn to friction
A little bit of sweaty mess is fine
Holding on to a silver lining
Holding a speck, stressed
Maybe it will be worth
When you lie with your hair caressed
Like strong fragrance, words can overwhelm Mistaken for a lousy
trick at a cheap show. However, they are a token of surrender,
The muse is the one who truly owns.

From A Nyctophile

My heart has a weird habit

it swells up and explodes sometimes

It comes out as poesies, silent tales to which I attach magic

More often than not,

night sky is a witness to it.

I feel the stars descent down

to console my tearing up soul

It lights up my darkness with heaps of hope,

My dampened spirits gets roused up.

I feel, night and me

Are meant to be,

Just like water and depth, or like the winds and secrets.

Leaving Home

Packing my life in card boxes
Memories flood my mind
As I leave the home I was born in,
Emotions I struggle to bind.

The walls that once held my laughter
Now echo with my tears
The familiar scent of the place,
Fades away as I fear.

The tree that stood tall in the yard
Where I played with friends till dawn
Now stands there, a silent witness,
As I leave it all and move on.

The creaky stairs, the old wooden floors
Each corner holding a story to tell
All now blur in front of my eyes,
As I bid them a silent farewell.

But as I step out of the door
Into the unknown and the new
I carry with me the memories,
Of the home I once knew.

So, here's to the old, and the new
To the memories that stay
To the nostalgia that grips my heart,
As I journey on, far away.

www.ingramcontent.com/pod-product-compliance
Lightning Source LLC
Chambersburg PA
CBHW020513160726
47991CB00007B/2931